WRIITE-
A PROCESS TO
FEEL; THINK;
GROW

Compilation of my Linkedin posts. A process to explore my way of thinking, feeling and growing. Key to my subconscious mind through writing.

SUSHANTA SAHA

ISBN 978-93-5610-208-8
© SUSHANTA SAHA 2022
Published in India 2022 by Pencil

A brand of

One Point Six Technologies Pvt. Ltd.
123, Building J2, Shram Seva Premises,
Wadala Truck Terminal, Wadala (E)
Mumbai 400037, Maharashtra, INDIA
E connect@thepencilapp.com
W www.thepencilapp.com

Author biography

Myself, Dr Sushanta Saha, from Asansol, is presently a resident of Kolkata, West Bengal. Assistant Professor of Physical Chemistry at Sree Chaitanya College, Habra. Graduated from RKMRC Narendrapur, 1999, with Chemistry Honours. Master's in Chemistry from Kalyani University,2001, Ph.D. from Jadavpur University, 2006.

Physical Chemistry Teacher; Personal awareness Counsellor |Reading; Speaking; Writing; Listening| Handwriting Analyst; Numerologist; Wristwatch analyst.

CONTENTS

Epigraph

Here on a journey to self-discovery through writing. The idea is to archive the change through a process called writing, speaking, reading, and listening. The context is my relationship as a learner, what I value. Clarity is a more important value than position, power, money, and it is writing, which is used to experiment and experience.

Chemistry can be medium of Self Discovery. Which will empower the learners. This writing is an initial step to How Chemistry can be used towards knowing self, and surroundings.

Let's begin with writing

Preface

The journey of myself is recorded here. During the Covid times, i was looking for avenues to uplift self, which may help my students in the process. The speaking challenge by Praveen Wadalkar created a space and context within me. Reading aspiration was enabled by Pavan Bhattad. Swami Sukhobodhananda, triggered Listening ritual. However, Harish Marnad, writing Challenge created a big shift in me. It tuned me to write my thoughts, watch my feelings, and grow gradually towards clarity. This book is dedicated to Harish Marnad, for his presence truly enabled me to reach out as a book.

Acknowledgements

The existence has its own reason to seek a receiver. I acknowledge the time, which I accepted, and with the blessings of my family, my students, and my departmental Colleagues in particular results happened. My wife, my daughter, with whom I shared my experiences of speak and grow app, truly helped me along the process. I acknowledge pencil for the support of publishing. The ms word, WhatsApp, LinkedIn, Grammarly, the mentors, the Digisol cable internet. Our home is a grand home due to Pisi, Rannar didi, and didi who help in building a healthy surrounding. I acknowledge my dada, boudi, Sagnik, and three dear brothers, Kaushik, Chiranjoy, Sourav Ganguly, two sisters, Priyanka, and Lipi. My financial planning and tax worries were addressed by Bipul da. Nabanita, my sister, and Mistu are always great in every way. My Dad always used to say, that ability is a poor man's wealth. Ma is a good listener. My late father-in-law, and mother-in-law, Chittaranjan Saha, and Bela Saha was always spirited and aligned to life and longing. The real environment along with the virtual interweaved a space of cognition.

I acknowledge all who have touched me all throughout my life.

Introduction

Journey of Powerwriter

We are all on a journey from consumer to creator. Dependent to Dependable status. Default to Design self.

The struggles and challenges are omnipresent. Within the challenges lies the opportunity for the prepared self.

Are we preparing, uplifting ourselves?

Noise is all around. Entropy never decreases.

Acceptance of the fact and cultivating beliefs is the way. My struggles include how I defy entropy by more inspiration than discipline. Use off PULL MECHANISM over the PUSH MECHANISM and support my students.

Discipline, methods do help us more to navigate the world with accountability. Fears get processed with the push from discipline.

The inspiration has a way that provides a flavor to the process. With inspiration, failure gets transformed into feedback. The creative understanding avails awareness of possible states.

I am a Physical Chemistry teacher and I am more oriented to observe invisible references, formless, and relate them to understanding. I have identified the role of surroundings that stabilize the system. I am here to culture compassion and uplift my being in the same surroundings.

Surroundings rich with Empathy, Authenticity, and Ingenuity will equilibrate more profoundly and gracefully. The virtual choice is now a fact.

The Workshop by Harish Marnad Marnad Sir is a 30 day Journey. The surroundings I chose for myself are to create more options for my students and also to connect with the idea of creating a Brand. I want to be the gardener who cultures awareness in the garden of colorful Chemistry.

The team of Harish Marnad, writing challenge, will support me with a new perspective. Inspire and contribute to writing something very different from Chemistry, realizing interdependence.

The #powerwritingchallenge prepares us to contribute, create, and connect the community with our own higher states of possibilities.

join https://lnkd.in/g3aaVvr.

My intro in the journey of this challenge was taken.

Direction of Intellect

Why Write?

We are all on a journey from A to C through B. Adversity to Circumstances through our beliefs.

Life is all about experiencing challenges with equanimity.

The education system is a way to cultivate skillsets to relish and connect in a more profound way.

.

The system (individual) is in equilibrium with surroundings and as per our surroundings, success gets defined.

Success can be money, market (quantitative). Success can be a relationship (qualitative, interdependence).

It is guided by only external forces when individuality is less realized.

Life has gifted us two things.

CHOICE and INTELLECT.

The choice is in abundance.

We need to increase, empower our intellect and make the right choice for smooth sailing and balancing. Writing helps us to connect and realize the beautiful connected state of clarity.

CBCS (Choice Based Credit System) system is a step forward in this regard to cultivating perspectives.

Comparing to Connecting is the way we need to talk more to create Compassion and a healthy self, family, society.

NO Where to NOW here

Rubick's Cube, How to look at a problem?

We are all on a journey from doubt to self-awareness. The journey is a summation of moments with choices that leads from circumstances to consequences. The turning points are invisible and meaningful with awareness.

2020, connected me with the three pillars of Learning. Speaking, Reading, and now into Writing way to the self-connectivity. I am into a 30-day #PowerWriterchallenge.

I will be writing considering learners, the 'WHY with HOW, Why the inner strength required for transformation. Discovering UNIQUENESS of each of the students, and how it can be realized within our Education system utilizing failure feedback. Connecting weakness into strengths. Introducing liking what we have.

Explore the world of learners, recognizing the passion within them, the superpowers. I want to share more perspectives. Then dive a little deeper into the consciousness of my students and be a compass of self-awareness.

I see the reversibility between Diversity and Unity in

Heterogeneity.

Students need a creative warrior mindset, and environment to blossom to see the invisible order in chaos. The need is flowing with life, rather than losing energy with competing.

I am in the celebration of confusion, my writing mentor is Harish Marnad, All members of this community are my support team members for the journey to build the ecosystem of interdependence through self-discovery.

Problems are awareness. The need is to look out for skills and connect with higher intelligence. Let infinite flow through this finite self.

Skill and Training- Process

Public speaking is a skill. Being a member of the #SpeakandGrow family of Praveen Wadalkar is a beautiful experience of networks.

I chanced to register myself with this community during the Lockdown. The 21 days of teachable introduced the idea of perspectives and activities, training continuously.

The assignment given to us was five minutes of talking concerning "How to build a relationship?."

Chemical bonding is very significant in Chemistry. With bond formation, energy gets released and stabilizes the molecule. Building a #relationship is analogous to bond formation.

Learning includes IQ, intelligent quotient, EQ, emotional quotient, SQ. The social quotient, SQ, is an essential component of growth related to bonding.

During my Hostel days, I have realized that the attitude of cooperation in studies is significant. The support from teachers, elders is common, available with awareness but less availed when at college. This lead to the understanding that the strength of the friendship is the foundation.

Sharing with classmates connects better, because of its reversible nature.

Here challenges of ignorance, doubts of I, personality and identity interferes, The pseudo competitiveness hurts the #bonding, interdependence.
This behavior in formal education hurts and breathes in all walks of life.

The SpeakGrow, the classroom is giving potential donors, the time to metamorphose from caterpillar to butterfly.
I am now with coach Harish Marnad

Awareness, Transformation, Navigation

Loshu grid and Numerology are very new to me. Sourav Ganguly, a friend of mine, provided me with the link to connect with the Arviend Sud community. The three relevant phrases I learned are AWARENESS, TRANSFORMATION, and NAVIGATION.

How this learning is useful to me?
Students are good and unique. Fire exists in wood, likewise, goodness exists in potential form. As a teacher, it's the creative challenge to bring out that goodness. (Fire is in the wood and when rubbed properly, the fire of excellence comes out)   ,

Our journey from NOW to the FUTURE.

Includes we are not happy now but will be happy later needs to be reduced in the process of change. Chemistry is about change, the awareness of the change that happens with learning. The Discovery of strengths, weaknesses can be a guide.

Strength to weakness and vice versa is about understanding.
The basic error is not the incident but interpretation;

awareness, and transformation.

The creativity to address, strength, weakness, need not be taken-for-granted. This is process-oriented, where satisfaction and laziness need to be surmounted.

Loshu grid of many students, friends, and relatives prepared by me helps me to be aware of my strengths and weaknesses. Strengths can be used to address weaknesses and repeated practice, habits can be cultured to translate weakness into strength, and transform.
It is the presence of digits in the date of birth, and the arrangements. (1 to 9 set) and its appearances in the grid that relates to the expression of muscles we carry.

11, in Loshu grid, is writing muscle, for me only 1, exists, stating challenges with writing.
I am into #powerwriting at Harish Marnad community, to address my weakness, transform them into strengths.

We @ RKMRC (1996-1999)

On my first day at RKMRC, Narendrapur, in the Ashram hostel. Awareness of West Bengal started pouring. Debasis Barik, Avik Sarkar, Ph.D., Arindam Gupta from Medinipore, Siliguri, DumDum, Sundarban, Habra respectively. Me from Asansol.

The first burst of water in the morning at 5 am, wearing a dhoti, Morning Prayer rituals are practices followed.

The age of Rebel cannot be denied, the attendance register records to maintain order in the system. It limited our vulnerabilities and flamboyant self simultaneously.

Life means the flow of experiences. Experience is the interaction between the Subject (individual) and the Object (world). It's thus a game for the REBELS. These plays are little acts of joyful tastes of hostel life.

The Khandano vaba and the music is a habit without direction unless inspired with meaningful interpretations. Awareness of rituals can multiply, magnify, sustain with creative perspectives.

The system of vibration is to magnetize the conscious and subconscious mind. The Bootcamp Warrior, MRM is similar training of habit to be in the present.

This pulling out from the past, entering into the anatomy of thought by sheer habits is also a means to multiply awareness, magnetize, and sustain.

#Powerwritingchallenge with Harish Marnad is likewise a TEAM to magnetize oneself and vibrate.

Waiting To Be Useful

If there is a student in you, the Teacher will appear.
Saraswati Yantra symbolizes a Seed multiplying into a forest.
A finite with the possibility of infinity. Devdutt Pattanaik, his storytelling sessions inspired me to connect mindfully with listening to stories.

Swami Vivekananda said, "You have to grow from the inside out. None can teach you, none can make you spiritual. There is no other teacher but your own soul."

Listening and reading are the two fundamental inputs for the
soul.

My personal goal is to resonate with a student and aligned with the direction to realize interdependence. Build a strong network with students. Create a system of interdependence and respect for each other.
Chandramouli Venkatesan, in his book Catalyst, mentions that we need a mentor to be more effective.

Numerology, Handwriting analysis a few crafts do correlate and outline strengths, weaknesses of students, and self.

How chemistry, concentration, old habits, relation in TEAM (Together Empowering To achieve More) connects, is an essential prerequisite for touching ends with means.

We have anger, we have an ego, jealousy, greed, lust, and the need is to look with creative perspectives to channelize. Need mentor, higher intelligence.

More than complaining we need to cultivate gratitude and need to replace toxic friends with coaches and good practice.

The need is to be open to the Universe and vibrate. #powerwriterchallenge

Failure!

I remember the 1st ArpitOnlineRefresher Chemistry Course. Scoring 10/10 even after listening to the video lectures was not a possibility for me. However, no restriction was imposed on the number of attempts to answer the questions.

Soon, restricted to 2 attempts midway in the course. This made me change the strategy to address the assignments. The aim is scoring, learning took back seat.

Previously I used to revise, relearn, which changed overnight. The goal 10/10 stood out.

Action is more important than perfection. Action helps with connections. Even if wrong it cultures effort. When there was no restriction on the number of attempts taking action and getting connected with learning was spontaneous for me.
A few of my friends shared that a restriction is essential, otherwise, all scoring 10/10 is never a true assessment of potential.

The goal is 10/10 and learning. Two attempts restrictions added. In the first attempt, I collected the questions and got them solved from Google or from my friends and enjoyed the 10/10 status.

The Flow zone of learning was self-sabotaged.

10/10 is the true conditioned reality. Unconsciously conditioned, my fears, decisions, past experiences, actions, and beliefs are the causes of my programming.
Results out of motivated action happen when all the causes team up positively.
Learning takes flight unconditioned.
Waiting, #powerwriterclub,   your perspectives.

The 3 Problems of my Prospects

1. Entropy all around: A disciplined external harmony of the system is missing in College Life. The awareness is essential to connect within to enjoy the pleasure of the pressure. The Why of learning is undecided and how of it is very superficial.

2. The self-talk: Unless one invests in learning and not doing the knowing. The application of knowledge out of passion and uniqueness of the being is the fuel to affirmative self-talk. The decision to set on a parallel journey for only a few minutes in a day will fuel the curriculum learning.

3. Average Mindsets: The mind can take over the matter. The Winner's mindset creation has the ability to work and achieve beyond ego. Achievement out of ego and comparisons will defeat the spirit in a team.

The problems are related to the connectivity of the subconscious mind with the conscious.
The need is to introduce a process and help them with the idea of how to learn along with what to learn. How imagination and association can enable one to remember

and create mind maps.

A system of habits needs to be created and directed towards goals that will enable one to receive creative perspectives in everyday learnings.

#powerwriterchallenge

Ideal state within Real states

An ideal state is a defined state of no interaction, where all particles are independent of one another.

We are all on a journey from our dependent self to our independent self (dependable).

The Kinetic theory of gas searches for properties of the system and establishes the relationship between, state parameters (P, V, T) to design a functional form.

We live in a relative world.

The back wheel of a bicycle is in a fixed state. The front wheel has the choice to set directions. With the identification of a problem or destination, the decision to direction happens.

The students who enter the system are each unique, have a distribution of specific traits. Idea is to set on a journey to realize their strength and identify the weakness to empower them.

TEAM-Together Empowering to Achieve More is realized in a system when the function is identified.

Amagat's curve, the plot of Z (compressibility factor, is a ratio of V of real gas to the V of an ideal gas) vs Pressure at a constant temperature is different for all gases.

The Pressure (stress) and how each gas flows at peace with pressure is realized at a particular T (Boyle temperature). The awareness of the state of being independent gets realized. The realization heals.#powerwriterchallenge

Movie Club

We are all on a journey to realize possibilities and in the process, experience ways to creatively dribble past resistances.

Be it metal conductor or conduction in solution the amount of current flow, I , is ratio of Voltage to Resistance.

Here in the domain of my prospects, resistance is limiting beliefs.

The mode of learning is essentially curriculum-based. Voltage is constant.

The how of learning and What is taken care of but the why has never been tried.
Extracurricular and Personal development is proportionately less entertained.
A few senior teachers identified and inspired to create a film club. Federation of Film Society, late Arunie Basu Roy paved the way.

I am the secretary of the film club. Usually, it's me who stay and connect, yet to reach out and catalyze the awareness.

Yet, I believe, College life needs to realize entertainment to enlightenment, a way to reduce self-blockages.

Mission Mangal, Soorma, Super 30, Gunjan Saxena, etc. can magnetize and attract and culture immense positivity with clarity.

The value is more important than money, position, power is beautifully portrayed.

Like #powerwriterchallenge, the power of watching needs to be practiced religiously. Entertainment to enlightenment is a journey to becoming.

To increase flow reducing resistance can happen with the cultivation of exploring new avenues.

Insecurity when inspires

I remember the 7 Day #powerwriterchallenge attracted me to register myself for Rs 99/-.

It is said you are the average of the five people you are with. Finding Harish Marnad offering ways to empower and build self-image and then personal branding helped me to connect.

With this challenge, my memory lane includes the two most beautiful English teachers in my school days. Late Mr. Gabriel of Class 8, said to me, "your English is horrible or terrible," with a sweet smile.
Mrs. Shalini Menon, Class 9. I owe her so much.

There are days when we get to connect and add value to the life of our students. If we get trapped in our technical aspect there is no system or team that exists to guide us.

To be predictable and consistent is the beautiful insight that touched me in this challenge.

The creation of a personal brand helps one to focus and know oneself. Experience self with expression.

In today's competitive world personal branding is not

about insecurity but it's an inspiration to look at oneself. Simplify to amplify reputation, STAR model. Success and fulfillment within getting interweaved.

What are your perspectives?

Biggest Insight

The GPS system identified, Gain, Pain connect to realise Solution system.

There are challenges, resistances intrinsic in any system. The idea is to communicate and harmonise.

The external challenges are mostly skill based. Internal challenges are usually limiting beliefs.

Here comes Harish Marnad to help and build a tribe. His message is simple and straight. Let the world know you exist.

How? He will enable the system, create a website, guide one to join dots and create patterns, and build a team where empowerment will be in autopilot mode.

Why? is for us to seek within. A quest to meet oneself. Communicate our offerings to the world. Identify the target audience. Take pain to find ways to solve and reap benefits for them.

This made me wonder, I am here for students and for

parents who are yet to recognise the strength within them. How I solve the puzzle? Try.

Challenges is not about actions and decisions but the sense of directions needs to be identified.

Time, Energy are core resources which gets affected if direction is not proper.

However the core assets for Teacher, trainer coach is the FOCUS. This challenge is helping out with knowing, figuring out vision, mission and narrow down, get focussed.
Try and fly

Imagine with me

I remember to join a 2-day webinar by Pavan Bhattad Institute of Thinking NLP on 6,7th November 2020.

How to read 100 books, 2021.

This introduced, how imagination with the association can be a wonderful tool for retention. The use of non-sense, a creative process.

Being a teacher, techniques of how to learn are useful. I shared the link with my students, friends, and families.
My wife said people will run away from you because of your preaching. My daughter says you are less father and more teacher. She has named me the webinar dad after engaging Saturday, Sunday.

The Foundation of memory is about Observations. Observing surroundings, collecting pictures, and connecting with patterns is a practice. This act of observation can be worked and be programmed once we know the ways. @StephenWiltshire is an example of how powerful our eyes can be.

The Visualisation aspect when included in learning, imagination pulsates. Imagination involving oneself and creating a story to remember 7 Habits by S Covey was a beautiful experience in the webinar.

Imagine and associating with oneself as doing, witnessing is beautiful indeed.

Parenting, teaching only get the least resistance when play; fun incorporates.

What are your perspectives?

Space and Time to space-time

"Manager! Manager!" A shrill and loud call from downstairs

My heart fumbled, set my specs, and dashed out of my hostel room.

PG Hostel II, Dining Hall, Kalyani University January 2000. Time at 11.30p.m.   ..

I realized something is not right and the heavyweights of the hostel have nothing to eat. Somehow we (Debasis, Asis Baruri) have wrongly calculated the number of meals. Pranab Da, Sudha da, Saptam da, Biplab Da has no rice.   .

We joined the PG hostel in August 1999 and as per rule, the newcomers must visit every room to introduce themselves. I decided to skip these four heavyweights since they were too heavy.

Today after 20 years when I connect with the night, I find they don't remember that they have lighted the fireplace with coal and prepared rice for themselves, acknowledged me.
They only asked for the storeroom key so that they can get

the rice.

We bonded and they prepared an omelet for me to celebrate the togetherness.

Today, they connect with more subtle, my words with them.

The journey from space and time has curved itself into space-time, relativity.

Omnipresent space and time lose the notion of absolute.

Relationship manifests likewise.

Lucky Escape

A two rupee coin seat at bottom of the bathtub is filled with water, the need is to drop a coin and hit it.
We alternately tried, but both our scores read, ZERO hits.

No success for both.

Dad, what is the magic behind #theLuckyEscape for the coin?

#LuckyEscape!

The year 1989, me too in standard FOUR. The fresh experience and riding cycle have earned me freedom.
On a particular day in the afternoon, I met with a fatal accident. I remember I was taken to the clinic, around 10 km from our home to get my right cheek stitched. My lips burst open and also required stitches.

A riding bicycle defined me as I could perform acrobats, and maintain high speed.

Taking a sharp turn near my home appeared disastrous. An uncle of our locality was about to cross and my speed of entry startled him. He was disconnected and responding to stimuli, he spontaneously got hold of my bicycle. The sudden break in the momentum threw me in a bad state.

Blood all over my face threatened. I was immediately rushed to my home. Neighbors dressed my wounds. My mother asked my elder brother to inform my father at Office.
All the uncles and aunties decided not to wait for my father. My mother was puzzled. A cab from the DPS (Disergarh Power Supply Co. Ltd., Jhalbagan, WB) company was managed immediately.

On returning home after dressing, I met with my father, family, and community waiting.
My father was thankful to GOD. Grateful for the support from our neighbors. For him, it was #myLuckyEscape.

Dad, you are lost in your world, my daughter complained.
Eureka, my coin struck I felt thrilled.
Coin of steel; Ship of steel, a same material different fate.

Archimedes Principle states that, when a body is immersed fully or partially in a fluid (water), it experiences an upward force.

Real and Apparent is always a game.

Gift

Life is a gift. Self-doubt, limiting beliefs must not stop one from growing, performing, and achieving all that is possible.

Bertrand Russel, wrote, "To teach how to live without certainty and yet without being paralyzed by hesitation, is perhaps the chief thing..." #inspiration,

I had the opportunity to meet Debasis Das, Ph.D., MBA da. We were having a great time with our learning and earning provision in the PG course at our college.

Debasis da decided to join the position of Associate Professor in the state of Gujarat.

After a year or two I, @Atanu Mitra da, Debasis Da celebrated a parting-togetherness party at his home.

He is returning to China.

When surroundings around asked him WHY?

From his words, he connected the Quantum Mechanics revolution of paradigm shift from certainty to uncertainty through action, decision, and direction.

By acknowledging Uncertainty, the deterministic reality dissolves and he recognizes that we are all in that soup, whether we realize it or not.

With him, I experienced that we should not resist pressure but rather flow with pressure and experience the gift called L(IF)E, with IF.

Mind over Matter

I remember the sound of the conch shell piercing the morning sky with sound and instructions, wake up! The conch shell vibrations are to catalyze the mind over matter.

Suvasika, my 9 y old daughter, woke up. It's time for riding.

However, the comfort is more profound, and to carry her mind over matter, I need TEAM to operate. From 7 am to 8 am, the TEAM oscillates to help her mind to win over.

The morning section of our college is for girl students. Most of them are obedient and follow instructions. Usually, all attend; still they too are distributed with their timings to enter the class.
Most of the students conveyed that they need to perform some other tasks to stabilize their system. I allow them with the message that consistency in the habit strengthens our minds, discipline liberates.

I enjoy this expression and connection with them since I believe that wisdom settles in day-to-day living.

The journey of, information to knowledge to insights and wisdom is a never-ending process. The ways to the spirit of understanding, are many and unique for all.

Waiting for your take on the significance of Mind over Matter with ... say 6 am challenge or something.

Real Education

A few days before, I was pursuing my daughter to get on her bicycle and learn to ride.

My job was to motivate and let her see the gain once the pain to learn gets embraced.

Today, I was running and panting after her bicycle. I was enjoying my moments of satisfaction. I could see the freedom in her speed and in the future canvas of my mind I witness her soaring high in the sky.

What is Real Education?

Real education from my perspective is to help one bring out the possibility. It is about loving what you do. It is about adding value and connecting differences. It is about helping the other to see the gifts one is born with.

Explore the fears, limiting beliefs, doubts, and find ways to a meaningful life for self and for all around.

At the very beginning, my daughter was afraid to leave the field and get onto the roads. She used to stop seeing any engine vehicles and used to avoid the rough patches on the road. Using her mask and breathing heavily would create vapor in her glasses.

I used to see her and smile. I shared with my wife that once she learns to ride well she will have no complaints with these external disturbances.
Education is a method to achieve a state of being, in which resourcefulness is interwoven to attain freedom.

Why Write

My wife asked me, Why do you write?

I asked her why do we use a thermometer?

Her response to my question is the reason I am writing.

You might be wondering, What is the relationship between thermometer and writing?

To answer this question, let's understand how a thermometer works.

A thermometer is a device used to record temperature changes. To record the temperature changes, three things are important:
> Mercury
> Glass
> Source
mercury and glass are part of the thermometer, as many of you know. When we place the thermometer against the source, the glass receives heat from the source and transfers it to the mercury inside it. As the temperature around the thermometer's tip called the bulb changes, the mercury rises or falls accordingly.

Likewise, our words are a result of the changes in our thoughts. Our thoughts are a result of our perspectives. When we express ourselves through our words, we show the world who we are. I see writing as an opportunity to showcase my personality and connect with others.

That is my reason to write?
What is yours?

Failure is Feedback

My 8-year-old daughter's eyes were bursting with tears. "I am a failure," she wailed.

When I slowly persuaded her to tell me what happened and understood that she had failed in her Google Classroom Arithmetic test. I hugged and said "It's okay"

Her cries grew stronger and then she told me the real reason she was so upset. She was worried about what her mother would say once she found out about this.

I realized her fears were directed more towards her parents than the failure itself!

As parents, We recognize their success with gifts and extra pocket money, but we fail to acknowledge their failure.

I reassured my daughter that her failure is not going to stop us from loving her. This time I saw her light up and she said, "I know I failed because I did not calculate properly. I will try not to do that again papa".
I could not be more proud of my daughter at that moment.

More often than not, it is not the failure but the fear of the consequences of failure that makes it seem larger than it is. Once we eliminate the fear, a large mindset shift happens with children. They feel comfortable discussing their shortcomings with us.

Failure is feedback, whispering to connect with higher intelligence.

Do you have a failure story? How did you deal with it?

Safety Pin

When does living disrespect the non-living?

To know this follow me, said the "SAFETY PIN" in the chaos of PG Chemistry class.

Me, the SAFETY PIN, is with a long strip of paper vibrating with discomfort. I am fastened with cloth, helping a long strip of paper to hang as a tail.

Now, sitting puzzled, in the palms of the girl, with teardrops and memories. The tears touched me with distress.

The differences in the room, newcomers, and old students surfaced.

The TALE OF A TAIL. The already students of the University unmindfully played the joke with a newcomer.

When does living respect the non-living?

I am a safety pin and my purpose is to fasten clothing together.

That day a magician from the newcomers appeared to arrange a glass full of water. Pulled out a James clip from his bag. Distorted the clip and placed me carefully in the water.

For the very first time, I was experiencing floating.

All the class was hooked to see my fate.

The SAFETY PIN floating and the class tension dissolving, with experiencing Surface Tension of water.

Non-living transcends the dimension of physicality. Building connections for conversations.

Google "Arvind Gupta toys", to enjoy transformations.

Toys from Trash.

A Memory

The year was 1988, and three days before Durgapuja, around 7 PM, the BSc exam results were declared.

"At this rate, I will never make it anywhere in life," said my friend Raj, in between his sobs. He was disappointed that he did not score as much as he had expected.
Next to him sat another friend Shubha who was trying to console Raj despite having failed the exam.

This scene is quite common even now. Students are not mentally prepared to handle failure. They get beaten up so easily and get derailed by a single setback. There are three main reasons for this.

Self-Awareness: It is very important to know how strong we are in a particular subject before expecting marks to come by.
Another factor that plays an important role is how well did we prepare for the examination. Unless we have worked hard, expecting results is not right.

Competition: It is a very competitive world out there, and missing out on opportunities has more probability than getting one. This clouds the heads of the students and does not allow them to see beyond the marks.

While it is good to remember that the competition pushes us forward, we must not get worn down by it and reduce our efforts.

What are your thoughts? How do you get over failure?

Personal Branding

My wife asked me, "What is Personal Branding?"

On searching within my thoughts, I remembered Praveen Wadalkar.

We are all on a journey to build relationships and Personal Branding is a way to connect the dots and complete our journey towards being a better communicators.

She left, but her question stayed.

I carried on introspecting or reflecting on the question asking myself what was in it for me?

I am a teacher. I have many ideas on how a student struggles to learn and ways to address the same. How do I communicate this with them? Personal Branding helps me in doing this by reaching out to students with my content.

A brand is not just a logo or company name. It is about aspirations, about the creation of looking glass beyond personal growth and figuring out what we want to see in this world with our content.

#PowerWriterChallenge is one of the best ways to tune

ourselves for Personal Branding.

How does this help?

It is all about writing and aligning our writing with our inspiration. Through power writing, you get a chance to:

> ignite minds
>create opportunities
> builds mindset of prosperity

Personal Branding is the best way of telling the Universe, What We want for ourselves from the Universe.

Winnie The Pooh- Noise is Fun

Some stories are so beautiful. Especially the ones that have a lot of hidden meanings are so wonderful!

If you've read Winnie the Pooh, you'll get the reference here.

To catch a bee and look for honey, Pooh ruins the garden that Rabbit so carefully nurtured and had grown. So careful that he would never let anyone walk that way and would not let even birds chirp there.
He isolated himself from everyone only to grow this perfect garden of his dreams.

He goes so far as to place a board calling for silence and orderliness. But, Rabbit realized something was missing.

One day he finds Winnie and other friends having a picnic and Rabbit, was not invited.

Nursing his hurt, Rabbit comes out to find everyone enjoying. There was no order and there was so much noise. That's it. That's all it takes to be with others: some noise and some fun.

Students are this way, too. Laziness, disinterest, and low

confidence level make them isolate themselves from others. However, with a little bit of fun along with the lessons, it is easy to help them realize that learning together is easy and not as intimidating as they had thought. Everything becomes easy when it is done together.

What are your thoughts?

Life is Uncertain

If there is one thing I know for sure, it is that Life is Uncertain.

When uncertainties strike, we realize our life's true value and how we are just passing away days without actually giving meaning to them.

What happened to one of my friends taught me a beautiful lesson on how precious our life is.

My friend Debasis Das, Ph.D., MBA was crossing the road at Jadavpur as he does every day when an ambassador hit him. It was a hard battle to fight and my friend came out like a phoenix from the ashes as a transformed man.

During his recouping period of six months, which he mostly spent as a bedridden patient, he noticed how he was always living for the future—making large plans and charts on what he must do at present to live the life of his dreams in the future.

As he was in the hospital looking at death, staring at his face all around, he understood that life has its way of hitting us hard. When it does, all we can do is accept the reality and move on.

In our continued efforts to live better in the future, we miss out on living at present. I will carry this lesson with me forever in life.

What was the biggest lesson that life taught you?

Build Trust

Shyam's eyes were red with tears as he entered the hostel room.

He could not believe that his student, who was in 8th standard, had taken his life by drinking Formalin.

He was so heartbroken about this and I wanted to reach out to him and comfort him.

When he decided to visit the grieving family, I did not want to send him alone and went along with him.

He recalled how bright a student he was and how he always completed his science projects on time throughout the journey.

He also felt that the student could have reached out to him in case he had any issues. He was crying and in between, he said something that took me by surprise.

Why did the student not trust him?

It is very hard to answer that questions as trust is not something that can be quantified. It can only be built.

Not all students are the same. Sometimes it isn't easy to connect with certain students. The best way to show them you trust them is by showing them that:
> You care
> you are willing to listen
> you are not going to judge
> help them see their shortcomings without being rude

Once the students trust us, it becomes easy to help the student and ensure that he does well.

What are your steps to build trust?

Love Story

Are you afraid of Sabita? I asked Swapan

Do you love her?

Don't expect that she will take the initiative; so energize your motion.

Channelise emotion.

FEAR of unacceptance and the consequences crippled my best friend.
FEAR creates noises. Noises interfere with energy.
FEAR is the friction, which saps away energy, and imagination is hijacked.

I decided to face it, create the way, and inspire.
Since I too felt similar FEARS is related to Sonali.

Me: Sonali, Hi!
S: Yes.
Me: I learned that your father is a very strict Chemistry teacher, is it true?
S: Why do you want to know?

Silently I told myself DDLJ and Amrish Puri matters.

Me: Is he ruder than Amrish Puri?

Everything around us stopped.

Me: No, If I get to ask for your hand?
This Love story did not materialize.

But when we resolve to meet our FEARS, we win because we learn to transform disappointment to discover our own selves.

Beauty in imperfections breathes life.
Isn't it?

Detox

My wife raised an important question.

How is the subconscious mind useful for students?

I uttered the word, "DIALYSIS."

My wife stood there giving me a puzzled look.

This took me back when my uncle was admitted to the hospital due to renal failure and he was prescribed to undergo dialysis, which means we had to shift him to a different hospital for the procedure.

We understood the importance of detox at that time as every minute was crucial.

Likewise, our mind is the kidney that acts as a toxin remover from our thoughts. Consciously, we have no control over our thoughts at a superficial level.

Understanding our subconscious mind can help open our way to organize ourselves better.

Every student has the possibility with himself to understand the subconscious mind and unearth millions of options.

Planting a very good seed in mind can lead to a beautiful garden of flowers, helping to become a better person.

Students today go through a lot of stress in terms of studies, career, emotional wellbeing and physical health.

If only they could understand the subconscious mind and manage it properly, it can do wonders for them in terms of both emotional and physical well-being.

Hidden Figures

Ask yourself and write your Goal.

I advised. The voices and noises started to unfold among my B.Sc. final year students.

We have no goal, sir. No purpose. We have not decided yet, what next?

Okay, I replied

Please, give it a try, even if vaguely something comes to your mind.

With this, I started to introspect, How do I energize and inspire them to see the blessings of the Universe?

Biographies, Real life stories, and short stories can help them to find the drive for their desire.

Hidden Figures is one of the must-watch movies which I strongly recommend to all my students.

This film is a great reminder to be resilient and not give up on self-belief regardless of the odds.

Here are my reasons why:
How the three female Afro-American mathematicians accepted their racial challenges, gender discrimination and fought through them is unbelievable.

These resistances exist everywhere for everyone. We learn so many skills as we progress in our lives. The difference between a person who succeeds and the one who does not lies in how these skills can improve our lives.

This film is a classic example of the same.

Self-belief is a small promise we make to ourselves every day. This little promise helps us to grow every day.

Examination at Hostel

The voice that sprang out of the mobile was exuberant. "How are you, Susanta?". It asked me.

I was taking time to remember the voice.

I identified Pallab immediately. Since I know he correlates me with all his academic success, I understood this must be one of those calls. Another milestone.

I was floating in the pleasant past memories we shared at the hostel.

My wife gave me a surprised look and asked Who called?

I replied VULNERABILITY and QUALITY. Her puzzled look told me she didn't understand what I was saying.

From Pallab's point of view, he was not expecting me to show up at his room and was planning to skip the Examination the next day.

When I walked in, he was convinced about skipping the exam and dropping out of college. There were also some of his friends who were convincing him to take the exams.

I decided to share my insecurities about the exam with him and how I had planned to tackle the same. I spoke to him, intending to motivate him to appear for the exams.

And he did appear for the exams. To date, Pallab thanks me for all his academic achievements and it is one Quality I cherish about him deeply.

I realized the Universe was ready to offer so much. Sometimes it is the restlessness within us that inhibits us from seeing beyond.

Smoking is a Choice

The cigarette touched my lips, and a smile flooded my face.

> Let me enjoy my smoking moment.

Niladri and me stranded in the bubble of noiselessness in the midst of noises. The moment with own selves.

The world, the society will not trigger unpleasantness.

No further explanations, part-time, phrase.
End of the endless frustrating queries.

We both are selected for the post of Assistant Professorship.
Identity recognized.
>Do you teach?
>Which College?
>Part-time?

The judgments, the measurements, the opinions of surroundings are in abundance. Unkind voices will now get defended automatically by the professional identity.

Freedom: a new adventure.
Journey to independence from dependence achieved.

Softly Niladri interrupted uttering a Sanskrit sloka
Mangalam Dishatume Akasha,
>What does it mean, curiosity in me asked.

Let SPACE bless us.
Physical, Psychological, Spiritual space.

We need blessings of space, a distance from self to witness
our contribution.
Space, for understanding our relationship with the other.
When you smoke you justify your carelessness towards
your immediate fragile ecosystem.
Someone can ask you to get the smoke at some other
corner.
What you allow to you, is choice?
Independence or Dependence.

Practice Awareness

The alarm with soothing music is on.
>5 minutes dad
Her mother was annoyed; every day my daughter stops the alarm and keeps sleeping.

>No more alarm clock from now, the annoyance carried with words, startled both.

I decided to intervene.
For me, the thought of rising early in itself is a remarkable decision.

Her thought must be supported.

The fact, if we throw positive thoughts in the air, the positive thoughts will land being useful, wherever it drops. It may take time but it will never hurt.

The process associated with waking early initiates with self-talk. Talking with ourselves is a critical and adventurous journey. It is a challenge for everyone.

Her mother's scolding led to sit her upright, immediately. Soon she was found with her harmonium. This self-effort is truly wonderful; obviously scolding accelerated the process. The journey of thoughts to doing is always appreciated.

Puja bells ringing, her Ma is with rituals.

The singing and playing harmonium inconsistent, I walked to meet my daughter, sleeping over, on the instrument.
I smiled and reached out. There is no way of escaping nature.

As individuals, we all have our inherent strengths, limitations. When we are honest about wanting to know and discover, we grow. The Key is practice & practice.

What is Tension

What is tension?
A simple question triggered stress, anxiety, and uneasy feelings.
Sir, tension is a force
>Two or more forces operating simultaneously at a point.

Everyday classroom tension of Q &A; feedback of ignorance, keep continuing.

Thoughts, feelings are automatically conditioned as per the class of the teacher.

I remember, our no worries with HKC sir's class. It had no baggage of worries since answers followed with questions.

RC sir can pick anyone from the group by name. Listening to that name generates sweetness within.
Sus, what reaction type is this?
Don't know sir, acted feeling sad.
This feeling of sadness will be substituted gracefully,
then know it, it is a substitution type of reaction, OK.

SM sir will pick you up, ask you to stand, will apply force, ask to turn 180• and ask the stereochemistry, the configuration of the molecule.

Everything around blurred.
The ways of the intellect were hijacked.

When such experiences occur frequently, feelings overwhelm. Pain becomes a problem. The thinking, feeling gradually conditioned to let down, self-belief evaporates.
How do we surf the turbulent waves?
skip the class.
learn beforehand?
write and pray OMG continuously.
Duck down and transfer yourself to a hiding position.
bear the pain.
suggestions...

Giving

Can you share your copy?

Yes, I can

I will explain the concepts, intervene another.

Being generous is an attractive trait. It reflects kindness.
Giving and receiving create joy within and it's not involuntary. One seeks, other accept.
I remember to misplace my exercise book before my exams.

Whom to ask?

Who will share?

Our teacher instructed and always inspired us to volunteer our learning with our friends in the group.
However, in the group, it was challenging but when one expands the boundary beyond, it's exploring.

Tuition was not an option for a few of my friends. They were eager to learn and appreciate the notes. This practice unknowingly helped me to discover my rough copy scribblings and it was a Eureka moment.

Today, I thank my teacher, Ashis Nag sir, for helping us to cultivate giving. He could have suggested don't share the notes with others.

When students team up and help one another, the feelings of compassion, empathy, gratitude, love creates ripples, and the attitude of giving is born.
Intellect may resist with questions, with Why? How?

Time, patience, and practice with a coach, can get it done.
Learning how to give informs us of the way to care, which gets translated into a giving mindset.
The Universe is waiting with abundance.

Application of Tension

"Early morning and you are smoking, S ?" A, quite puzzled

I quoted, "SMOKING IS INJURIOUS TO HEALTH."

S, responded, Releasing tension.

Exam tension dilution? I smiled.

No, and Yes! Somewhat. Need the feel, Build the tension of exam and thereby smoke.

I never experienced or heard someone admitting counter to the normal feelings regarding the examination.
A: pushed me, directing me not to linger around S on this topic. We dispersed.

We were all back at the hostel by evening.
S, how was your exam?
BINDAS!

The fundamental requirement to address any #examination is #confidence. Thinking positive.
However, for S, thoughts of fear w.r.t questions forgetting the answers during exams, or making trivial mistakes do not intervene. He could build himself believing and

visualizing the larger picture about himself beyond immediate challenges. He used ways to pick, cultivate positive thoughts, and likewise programmed #subconsciously.

What are your suggestions and ways before the exam?

Make a Wish

Please turn on the radio. Asis pursued
But, Jayanta, may feel disturbed. I informed.

Lower the voice and we can listen to the conversation, it's
very interesting, It will help us all.

I handed him the radio.
The idea of the conversations, with songs in between, was
related to wishes.
If God asks us to wish, that one wish will be fulfilled.

What will be the wish?

A good Job
A good research career.
Acceptance in love.
Address Poverty
Address corruption ...
All started pouring but no forms seem to satisfy the
seeking within.

Asis asked me, your wish?

I wanted to be more smart and specific.
I was pursuing Research in Chemistry also an IAS aspirant,

not aligned.

I want to be a tool through which the grace of God can reach out to people, want to be an IAS officer.

This seems two if you want to reach out, being yourself is enough, Asis included.

Single wish seemed less to empower me.

I asked Asis, what do you wish?

Asis, said I will ask God to carry me to that goodness which God thinks is good for me.

He supported his want, with more references and experiences.

What appears good for us, say our love for a girl may not be appropriate in the long run.

Praying for material form does help us but the formless heal us.

The journey begins with wishes.

Wish

Write

May I come in?
Yes.
Sir, May I …

There are two ways to catch the class.
>Get before the class
Or
>Get late

The solution is to be on time, cultivate the habit
>wake early
>cooperate.
>prepare do list before

I allow each student whenever they feel to join the flow. My classroom is my TEAM.
It has a Goal to achieve. We need to score marks, also need to have the feel of success with three essential teammates joy, happiness, and satisfaction.

How to deal with latecomers?

The reward Punishment model does exist in the system to cultivate discipline. However, I feel that the distribution of all coming needs to be respected. Judging diversity will drain my own resources, time, and energy.

Now, how to score marks?

I suggest five habits.

>Habit of reading question papers
>Habit of searching for answers
>Write them
>Archive them
>Share with your friends

Foundation is Write, Write, Write.

Writing is the key to the subconscious mind. The regulator
is essential to control, fans and AC.
Likewise, writing is the regulator, which helps us to control
rightful information from the vastness of available data.
Writing process learnings with structure.
Writing channelize the mind towards the direction.

What more habits, do you recommend?

Miracles

Prove, NOTHING = NOTHING, A, asked all mischievously.

This triggered explanations and interpretations to roll out in abundance.

I transported myself sitting at Asansol, in a bus, fighting with desperation for a water drink.

"#Burnpur; #CourtMore.", a repetitive call out from the conductor of the bus, for more passengers to flow in.

I, returning from the hostel with the realization of suffering at the moment, due to my two best friends Procrastinate, and Laziness. Forgot to pack a bottle of water, check my purse for the journey ahead.

Sitting beside the window witnessing the layers of challenges unfolding out of my laziness.
Dad asked me to get my bag packed in the evening.
Ma asked me to set the alarm rightly.
The youth in me with two special roommates, EASY and FUN skipped all suggestions.
Now, at the moment, NOTHING equates to

NOTHING. Third law of Newton is every action with an equal reaction.

Thirst within me suddenly located a man wandering just outside the bus near the window where I was sitting.
Desperate! Yet, shy! asked for water.

Tasted bliss, called LIFE.
How much do I pay?

NOTHING, he signaled silently and vanished.

NOTHING = SOMETHING.
#Experience transported the observer in me witness the #Miracles in THE same MOMENT of LIFE.

Direction

The volunteers, in the midst of hundreds of followers at #SriSriRamakrishna's birthday celebration. The students, teachers, and all volunteers with specific roles manage the crowd of anna dana rituals. The premises of the ceremony at RKMRC Narendrapur.

S, pulled me to draw my attention.
> What?
> We need to move out?
I stood askance, puzzled, liberated.
> We will be asked to collect the leftovers, we have served a batch, we will silently leave.
Instantly transported into the drift of doubts, fears, indecisions.
The principle of Newton's First law in motion started to act.

An object at rest or in motion will continue to be at rest or motion, and direction, unless acted on by an unbalanced force.

#AVS sir, the then HOD of our Chemistry
department was into action, collecting the remnants. His strict, disciplined way, his image all dissolved to embrace us in Togetherness.

> I nudged S, Direction installed.

Inspiration with action is more creative than Instruction to act.
The filled mind of youth when creatively pushed Formed mind get designed.

Internal force silently sets in momentum when the value gets added.

Pranam Sir.

Any leadership, and push you remember?

Frankness

Sir, Can I ask you something frankly?

What? I responded to the Whatsapp message.

Is it essential for boys to masturbate? Please help?

The challenges with instinct and intellect are so critical that it needs more perspectives to accept, acknowledge, and move beyond the physical.

I remember, G, rushed into my hostel room and confided in me how miserably he failed to converse with his student when he discovered the fact.

Sus, do you know, the sperms of my student were scattered around.

How do you know? I asked

I visited early today, and his parents were at the office. Nothing more is required.

How did you address it?

I said nothing. G felt shy.

To address the issue, knowledge, skills, and values associated with the event help the adolescent.

My crisis! It was created and we were a gang of class 7. Exploring, our ways to physicality.
With the realization of my class scores and weakness, I confided to my elder brother. But dreams started to create confusion.

Personally, met Dr. M, also went to my mother. The mother then told my father and the father thought I need counseling.
I was asked to practice GOMUKHASANA.
I texted, the chemicals, thoughts, feelings create waves and swift us but when we learn to surf in the turbulent waves we manage to reach the coast. Need direction, activities, engagement.

Ignorance, confusion, and guilt associated with private life keep fighting and defeating.

The metamorphosis from caterpillar to butterfly is waiting to be experienced and realized.

Life Skill

N, continuously crying out his heart out, "I want to go home."

Skip the Examination, Why?

Feeling embarrassed and disturbed to find my batch mates so insensitive to a friend who has come to a long distance and is suffering in isolation. Whom do I explain and communicate the challenges, N is struggling with?

The other side has another story. They have identified, analyzed the shortcomings of N, and in the final year, they have designed to disturb his center.

7 days gap before the exam; panic, and worry need to dissolve.
N must leave, I supported his decision.

Can I bridge, but no one is ready to listen.

What skills do we need to cultivate and surf the waves of unacceptance?

We all have bouts of pressure and we usually fail to anticipate, accept the thrust it holds. We are not introduced to Life Skills during our journey.
Life skills are skills that do not make a person look good on paper, but they assist in the steps along the way.

What are they?
> Emotional intelligence, more sensitive towards others
>Not being judgemental
>Staying calm in the face of adversity
>Art of communication
>Ability to face failure
>Good listener

Mutual respect and wanting to learn and grow are the bedrock of togetherness.

What more life skills do you suggest?

Time Machine

Think of 3 events of the past that you want to rectify?

Repeated the #TimeMachine operator.

You, S, get prepared.

Third in the row to enter TM.

Still to decide, puzzled,

>I attempted to take my life.
>I locked my mother outside the house.
>I broke the racket hitting my friend.
>I threw things at my best friend.
>I was thrown out of the exam hall.
The list goes on…

Which one to rectify? Why do I want to rectify seems to challenge me?

Decided
>To go back and share the water with the boy which my father denied thinking of me.
>Go back, appreciate and wear the wristwatch which my father purchased for me.

>Go back and share the entire poetry notes with T before the exam.

We do have #challenging and complicated lives and the personal journeys have never been easy and straightforward. We all have disasters and triumphs. These imperfections
are #opportunities for #cognitive reappraisal   which reframes references and generates empathy towards life.

"In the midst of crisis, lies great opportunities." Albert Einstein
This crisis cultivated and taught me to remain grounded in humility.

Thanks, TM, I can skip for now and allow others to discover their past.

Your thoughts, on the 3 events?

Science is Vision

S: Why, no practical class Sir? student enquired

I: T.C. meeting, at 12 noon, check the notice board.

S: Now it's 11 am only.

I: None of your friends informed you? After how many days you are here to attend class?

S: Tomorrow there was no Practical class so I was absent.

I: Why do you skip theory classes?

S: Do not feel inspired, but attend tuitions outside.

I: Try to be with class; classmates also. Togetherness is the key to sustainability.

He left but the words of the outspoken student kept me occupied.
There are many ways to home, likewise many ways to learn Chemistry. More ways usually help, but for him, it's TUITION only.

Each individual is unique, as each electron.

The electron has complementary qualities, similar to the wave-particle.
Similarly, each individual is docile and rebelling simultaneously.

It is for us to be alert and act accordingly to find direction.

Science could be the best rebellion against poverty, economic injustice, ugliness, and lead the way. Fire is in the wood.

The rebellious temper of skipping classes' for effective tuition notes, for a good score, as the only value defeats the system of learning Science.
Science is more than a score.

Science is Vision.

How do we walk in that direction?

Need to talk.

Sell Chemistry

What to sell? Why so tensed? P asked

I meekly said, tomorrow we have an interview for Assistant Professor.

P: They will ask you a simple question, WHAT IS CHEMISTRY? Why worry?

He left and kept me wondering, it's an #inspiration, #motivation, #introspection?

After completing my Ph.D., this inquiry is truly relevant at the same time challenging.

SELLING CHEMISTRY.

#CHEMISTRY is the dance of #OPPOSITES to celebrate #CHANGES.

Nothing happens in chemistry without energy being involved. The atoms that constitute matter do not change; only exchange partners and rearrange. Chemistry is all about divorce and remarriage.

The variety of opposites,(A, A'), set A and its complement, A'

> Energy; Matter

>Order; Disorder

>Loss; Gain (redox)

>Finite; Infinite
>Variant; Non-variant
>Available; Non-available free energy.
>Beliefs; Facts (Principles)
>Raw; Processed

...

Through love, we can bring the Synthesis between the opposites.

Atoms and Energy are two great rivers in Chemistry. The banks of the river appear apart but below the rivers are connected, $E=mc^2$.

A and A' = Universal set.
A or A' = Null set.

Chemists build bonds, create relationships, add value, and sell.

As Good and bad, bonded wisely carry electricity.

We are transformers to that direction of growing.

Slang

"Bull shit or Bloody fool" which has more weight." I enquired.

GOAT! You are playing with slangs, C impulsively uttered.

I: Why not? You have so many dynamic followers, Why not me?

Social interactions within a group grow with the informal use of words. Uniqueness, Space, and connectivity liberate.

C: But you are "Bhadralok"(descent). Take care.

Friends tell you, what you are good at. Again, circumstances demand to be accepted in the gang, failing to listen to the truth is desperation for acceptance.

Incompleteness within chooses direction.

BBC radios are good messengers. All groups have one.

BBC broadcasted that I am no more passive player, rather expressive and growing steadily with my community

vocabulary. Only the manifestation needs more tuning.
When we stay long enough and practice, the experience reaches a critical state.
We need a Friend, who will push the frustrated insider to either towards or away from our own being.

F: Slangs do not gel with you, drop them as early as possible.

It is easier for others to see what we ourselves can't see.

Listening liberates.

Connection to inner truth needs conscious listening to substitute, Connection to outer truth.
Are you listening?

What inspire you

What, you do?
I steer dreams to direction, I teach Physical Chemistry. Tell stories and give visibility to the invisible.

Why do you do, what you do?
I cultivate #SELFBELIEF in learners, students.
I tried CA, IAS, accepted for post-doctoral research but chose to meet KOLKATA.

All felt FAILURE, MYOPIC.

KOLKATA, inspired me to cultivate #COMPASSION, realize #empathy and connect.

Fear and hurt, resides in every one of us, but students open up, acknowledge the lower conscious selves more easily.
Mindful of the feelings of unworthy, complaining, frustrating, depressing emotions soon becomes the internal guide, with the help of empathy.

I enjoy building relationships with myself.

What inspires you about your work?
I am an #architect of the future. I learn when I teach. It is

said nothing is more gratifying for a teacher than finding a seeker who is ready. While it is true that, "When you are ready your teacher appears."

I am ready to be guided by my inner guide of frustration, complaint, victim, irritability, inadequacy, seeking love than giving it.

They all are now my guides from beyond.

Life is greater than what we are and my inspiration to work is to acknowledge #gratitude and match its vastness through contribution in my own way.

What inspires you?

Light

The wick dipped in oil, will get lighted.

Let's get the USG report, my wife said lighting the evening lamp.

Don't worry, I will get it tomorrow, I said tuned to the TV.

Again it will be the repetition of the same, her voice carried the weight of negative consequences.

The cup with a thin layer of coffee seemed to stare at me wanting desperately to communicate something. Something is drying up within.

I shifted my attention, what did you pray? Hoping, praying rejuvenates.

Why do you ask? She probed.

No answer to offer.

Repeated unexpected results have a pattern, non-acceptance.

We can adopt a child and be parents but decided not to

discuss this sensitive issue abruptly.

The USG report was handed in, we sat together, responded and discussed our concerns with the doctor, and came out together.
Trees surrounding the clinic have disallowed lights. India vs Pakistan World Cup match has all the light.

We both walked out in the open darkness, our hands clasped, she danced with ecstasy.

The two hearts struck, lamp within us lights hope.
The sweetest moment ensued.
The wick when gets struck by the bitterness of life can ensure light only when dipped in the oil of prayer, grace, and gratitude.

With LIGHT, feeling LIGHT.

Kaleidoscope narrative

Did you see the huge PG syllabus included in each semester?

Is it possible to complete the same within such a short period of time?

This triggered discussions considering the challenges and opportunities hidden within the Choice Based Credit System curriculum.
The World manifests as black; white, right; wrong. Comparisons are the key to debates and discussions.

In between the debate and discussion where our actual audiences stand, our students. How do these discussions give wings and help them fly? Which direction liberates?

How every face in the college could be acknowledged?

Do offline, online components unite and are useful?

I see two ways to Home. One towards the home and the other away from home. When I accept the challenge of uncertainty it's an adventure. With non-acceptance it's fear.

Administration, teachers, parents, and students are TEAM of learners.
When each of us live our lives with grace towards those around us, feeling free and enjoy the freedom to be ourselves. We move from the dichotomy narrative to the Kaleidoscope narrative.
A shift to creator narrative is an essential basis to transcend comparison.

Teachers create dissolve outlines.
The way from knowledge to understanding is the road to becoming.
Choose Creativity.

Pratul Chandra Rakshit Sir

I remember, Pratul Chandra Rakshit Sir, around 87 years old. He was the teacher of our Chemistry teachers. He frequently visited the Chemistry department at RKMRC Narendrapur, all students used to be around sir and listened to him.

I could not reach close enough in the department to offer my Pranam. At an annual prize distribution function, he asked all students to find the time. The time of around 15 to 20 minutes, every day. This is to invest in READING and LEARN something other than our respective honors subject.

The TOI, #TheSpeakingTree column, is still my READING practice.

In the year, 1998, he left us. His words ring and after twenty years I realize how his words touched me and helped me grow.

The journey from thoughts to things is a LONG ENOUGH process. Formless to discrete Form meets many good souls

>writing, now Harish Marnad

>reading PavanBhattad
>learning: an exploration

The faceless student, at one deep corner, remembers sir.

Great Teachers are like prisms. They have the power to see the light within each student. They catch that light to bend the beam and create a splendid spectrum of a rainbow. We all are unique spectrophotometric substances, with unique peaks.

Our spectrum has a peak to pick.

The REAL self.

Did you find yours?

Power Writer Club

On which side of the street is the #PowerWriterClub, Left or Right?
One can afford to answer when the direction of reference along the journey is known.

Who is bigger, PW or PWC?
It is hidden within, #TheoryofRelativity. The reference, angle of view, where one stands.

What are my learnings?
This 30-day #powerwriterchallenge has taken me on a ride, from thoughts to things.
Writing my thoughts guided by Harish Marnad cruised me through the forest of my mind and helped me navigate the space with limiting beliefs.
It created #Awareness.
The beliefs which processed my conversation during writings are created by my thoughts, reflected my mindset.
The #consistent approach to writing paved the way for my #Transformation.

What changes did it bring?
It has initiated momentum, new logical understanding, new feelings, new opinions, and new convictions.

Yet to arrive at the destination, the decision was taken justifying direction to growth mindset from a fixed mindset.

PWC is the surrounding, which is necessary to motivate and regulate my thoughts of my system. Together we create THE THOUGHT UNIVERSE.

#Einstein, aptly said, "The world as we have created it is a process of our thinking. It cannot be changed without changing our thinking."

PWC is the factory of thoughts with Vision.

Play with me

It's 6.30 am in the morning,
"Oishi wake up now? You have school HomeWork, sir's HomeWork, singing to practice."

Her mother is determined to cultivate the habit of rising early and help her eat the frog (idea). Difficult task first.

When did she wake up?
Around 7 .10 am, she left her bed.
She is physically fresh, energetic but demotivated because heavier urgent tasks are too much waiting for her.

Her father is two steps ahead of her. Struggling with managing time. Forming habits to write, read, speak and listen. Creating patterns with challenges like,
#powerwriterchallenge
#readingchallenge
#GoalFocologyy.

Her mother left for her school, asking her for 9 years to complete the tasks.

She came to me and scribbled on her hand, PLAY WITH ME.

I felt nothing to be discouraged. To surf, the waves of time the training begins with AWARENESS. Learning to be aware of time can be spontaneous, organic way. The other disciplined way.

Time is a resource, for me playing with her may stay with her.
Let's PLAY, TIME IS VALUABLE. ENERGY is valuable.
Channelize.

The direction of Time Management, and then to Mastery, begins with baby steps.

Struggle to AWARENESS.

NOW PLAY.

Notice your value

Do not waste time, this warning stays echoing.

This one-way street has been conditioned to such a degree that challenging it, creates doubts, and draining of energy.

The basis of any learning is questioning. I had the intelligence to question but the form was undefined.

I remember, English, B.Sc. Examinations at RKMRC Narendrapur we
were given a single day's leave for preparation.

"I am going to Nandan, anyone wants to follow," I said appearing confident. I decided to watch an English movie.

I went alone.

WHY AM I DOING THIS? Kept hammering me until I covered 19Km.

I kept thinking that saying NO to oneself sometimes favors more than saying YES.

The idea of doing less and achieving more was my intent. In the process found a new kind of awareness regarding

TIME.
When we scatter time, somewhere this very awareness creates a FOCUS towards TIME.

When I returned, my focus on learning increased. I started to hear my voice within me pursuing me and carried me away from gossip. A space for self-reflection gets created.

When the opinions, expectations, and obligations of the world around us are shut out, we begin to hear ourselves.
What we value gets noticed with our actions.
I valued disorder in the one-way order. I initiated a way to feel TIME.

Probable Pathways - Plan

We are all on a journey from the Present to the Future,
a journey from reactants to products.
Chemical Kinetics in Chemistry outlines the probable
pathways to the goal.

Sir, why do we study Chemical Kinetics?
To gain TIME.
What to do once we gain time? I asked to answer
We increase our productivity. The rate of reaction can
be increased as per our need.
We can control. We bring certainty. The aim of doing
more in less time gets fulfilled.

Sir, we want to study less but score more. Is it
possible with Chemical Kinetics?
With Knowledge, it is not possible but with
understanding it's possible.
Chemical kinetics dictates the speed and the
parameter of interest is TIME.
Skills, hacks, tips, mentors help.

As a student, I used to study for more hours than my
friend, yet scored less.
The value of 1 hour within many hours depends on
who uses that one hour and how one uses it.

D used to start his day with a plan.
>Highest impact things first.
>Outline question and answer
>Reverse learning; associate with imagination.
>Connect to mentors more often.

Mentors who are fulcrums (positioned at middle), they balance knowledge and understanding.
To do more in less time, the need is to shift, a fulcrum to understanding. A load of huge knowledge will get lifted inevitably.

Dad and Sir

1997, with my father before HOD Chemistry RKMRC
Narendrapur
The only query Sir has,
How do you justify 32 out of 150?
No answer.
Are you confident to score more on the next test?
I have studied, written all answers, yet…

#Selfconfidence is about our own ability to do something,
the measure of our own faith. But scoring low has
produced feelings of frustration and anxiety. So, yet…
hangs in the air.

Sir, prescribed recognizing my learning difficulty,
>drop a year
>try other subjects.
My father has traveled 250kms, will return after this
encounter, the light within me eclipsed.
Light by itself has no sense of failure; light does not take
anything personally. Circumstances cloud thoughts,
feelings, and emotions.

My father handed me the letter with the scores.
Keep it nicely, this will be oxygen for many.
I know you always try. Listen to your Professors, respect

them, and follow what they suggest. Bounce back.

My father carried a soft smile.
My self-esteem was boosted with that touch of words, with so much belief for me. His words kindled my subconscious mind and allowed me to feel my own self. Parenting can be simple when one has the capacity to look at failures and help one recover showing them the light within.

Contributing to #SelfEsteem.

Fear a Force- Use creatively

Buses have arrived. We will be carried to our UG Exam. Centre.
>Reserve my seat beside you, D called out from the Prayer hall balcony.
The Conch blowing and the ritual marking of sandalwood on the forehead were performed.
Seeing D praying triggered the conscious self to go back and insulate self to any negative vibrations.
The seat in the bus needs to be occupied; decided to let go of praying.

The FEAR is a FORCE. Any amount of revision and preparation cannot resist the creativity process of fear.
Anyways to offset fear?
D joined me and asked,
Close your book, just focus on your breath.
Which prescription to follow:

my own; continue revising
or
that advised.

Restless self, fear within me; created a hurt body.

Bus rolled.

Secretary Maharaj, boarded our bus at the RKMRC Narendrapur Gate.

The idea of detachment to outcome by him insulated the fear completely. The devotion, discipline; the dot-at forehead. Intuitive mind references were mysterious blessings to inspire us all.

The body leaves but something lives. His words meaningfully ring within me.

We are connected by invisible spiritual forces and visible events confirm.
The higher centers in us are constantly communicating to us, the need is to open us.

To fill the cup, turn it up.

Receive Grace.

Meditate

Could you be accountable?
Do you think you can fly anywhere with your final year
wings? Warden Maharaj has many queries.
In the darkroom of my mind,
I am looking
>for light
>for friend
>for breath
>for miracle
I have skipped the mandatory morning prayers and
meditation sessions.

Are you looking for a miracle?
The more effective way is to train yourself to embrace
miracles.
But, first recognize, be aware of the Miracle.

Sit down.
Think and tell, why do you meditate?

Ok,
first
How do you meditate?
>Count from 1000, in reverse.
>Visualise someone, a person, or the flame. I usually

follow first.

How do you feel after you meditate?
>Balance.
>Feel calm.
True, when we meditate we cultivate balance, awareness.
Look at the Sun, it gives light and also warmth. The warmth cultivates Love, Joy, and Kindness.
Likewise, meditation is light and cultivates awareness, warmth by controlling the breath.
By controlling breath we can control emotion, focus on the present, raise energy.
Breath is the pathway.
Even in sleep the BREATH only guards and keeps vigil to our LIFE.
Breath has so much to offer.
It is a magical tool, accept and shake hands,

Marking present in the attendance register proves your presence but I want you to improve and not prove.
Embrace Miracle.

The One

Do we all have Goals?
Do we all have Plans?

When I talk to my students, and with my friends they are confused.

Short term; Long term.

In the classification of types,
Career, Health, Relation, Finance, etc.

If I try coding listening to them, I find more ZEROES than ONE.

Emotions

What does ZERO signify?

Zero is anything invisible.
Zero by itself has no value, no meaning. Again without it,
Life is meaningless.
Zero is about
>Feelings
>Passion
>Vision

But how to hear and tune oneself to the inner voice. How to channelize the inner energy?

Today, we all are overwhelmed by external attractions. Where all-around achievements, 1.
Need is to interweave 1 with 0.
Creating understanding and awareness of energy can happen with positive catalysts, mentors, coaches,1 around.

Alignment with external coaches,1's will help to connect gradually with the internal coach.

THE ONE within.

1 is insignificant after 0.
(000...1)

With understanding and awareness; ONE before ZERO, mutate ZEROES to HEROES.
(1...000)

Are we aware of the PURPOSE?
Are we aware of the PAIN?
Choose your Goal, your Mentor.

The Team

M: Oishee, has found interest in Maths.
I: That's great news for us.
M: Her tuition sir has made it possible.
I: Great!

M: What are you doing?
I: Finding meaning in distribution?
M: What is that?
I: Story of two TEAM, with different effectiveness. Which TEAM is more effective.

M: TEAM?
I: Together Empowering to Achieve More.
< Mn > and < Mw >, are the Number and Weight average of Molecular Weight and used in Polymer Chemistry are the two TEAMS.

M: Can you elaborate?

I: Assume Knowledge is proportional to age. Then in a class of 50 learners, all learners are of the same age say 25 years(y).
The average for TEAM is 25y.
M: This is TEAM A?

I: Yes, likewise substitute 2 of 25 y by 2 of 10 y.

M: TEAM B formed?

I: No, we again substitute 2 (25 y) by 2 (40 y).

M: Eventually, 4 learners (25 y), substituted with other combinations, equal100y.

I: Yes, the Average of both Teams is 25y.
Knowledge of 40 is the key.

M: What is your intention with the calculations?

I: If a Common Challenge is arranged. TEAM B, which has distribution, from 10y to 40y will be more effective than TEAM A and win the Test.

M: Success and failure do not depend solely on self but it's the TEAM that matters. This is the message.

I: Yes, distribution in The TEAM. Together Empowering to Achieve More

Buddham Saranam Gacchami.

Counseling

Voice messages from an unknown number left unattended. Decided to listen while waiting outside my daughter's class. It's from a student who has dropped his 2nd sem CBCS exam, with reasons. Created YouTube channel. Looking for initiating a business for money. Will appear for Medical entrance.

I decided to call.

Asked his name and his DOB.

This partly helps me to outline the muscles he carries with him through numerology.

Found presence of intuitive muscle, deep insight muscle, writing muscle; at the same time restless.

He has the potential of a steady horse, presently he is on a sloppy track.

I asked him to define his expectations.

He wants to succeed in the medical entrance.

He has created a problem with his intellect. Overwhelmed with the surroundings. Wants to succeed, direction not defined, hence the drift.

Intellect is a knife.

A thief, a doctor both uses a knife, according their intellect, choices get oriented.

I asked him to realize the resources he has, the gift of muscles, anything unused decays with time.

As captain of the ship, has a compass. Likewise, identify the goal you want to reach. Create a routine to flow.
Take tuitions of science rather than opt for business.

Without getting things within us right, nothing outside becomes right.

Online and Offline

How are your Online class Exams? A, enquired
An email has been created to collect and distribute the
answer scripts to teachers.
OK, learning a lot.

All are scoring huge, do you call this examination?
How long do you think this drama will continue? The critic
within A surprised me.
Seeking minds are skeptical, but it appeared to lack respect
in the process.
We are in the midst of the Covid - Voting Festival.
Democracy accepts disagreements, differences but under
the basic rules of cooperation. I decided to take control of
the conversation.
I am enjoying my journey with Graphology? Each
handwriting has something to say about the mindset of the
student.
With looking at the script I get to know,

Who takes risks?
Who wants to make his identity?
Who values relationships?
Who utilizes time towards success?

A seemed not satisfied, "You have space and time, and how this is helpful for students?"
Yes, being useful for students is significant.
I am learning and enjoying the process. I said
So, you and your students are enjoying, A rudely analyzed.

Frankness in itself is never a problem; it is bluntness with our frankness that when expressed, makes a difference.

Difficulties do not crush. Ignorance does.

Ignorance creates Fault lines, miss macro in micro.

Hence miss respect.

Eradicating contempt is truly challenging.
Opinions?

Boundary and Limit

I will throw away the mobile. Oisi's mum yelled. Continuously watching; damaging eyes, and as a dad, you say nothing to her.

The concern is meaningful. I should say something to Oisi.

But again confusion within me leads to hindrance in peace. The family struggles.

Obsession with mobile does not allow energy to be stored for action. The mobile Activity takes away the energy for Action.
I want my daughter to inculcate habits to substitute mobile.
As a guide, I inspire to

Write, Read, Speak, Listen

But the system stabilizes when the surrounding is stable.

Oisi, adds doubt into the stability,

YOU BOTH SPEND HOURS WITH MOBILE.

True.

The statement triggered annoyance, hindered peace.

One assumes she is crossing her LIMITS.
Mobile cannot be avoided by us, for reasons.
Now.
For me, it's the conflict of two similar, but utterly contrary concepts of LIMITS and BOUNDARIES.

LIMIT is the endpoint of one's reach for freedom.
Without freedom how can one grow?
The BOUNDARY is positive. One cannot have a boundary without there being something real beyond it.

The Limits turn differences into offenses.

Silence can be forced upon to LIMIT.
But with understanding, with cultivating interest, grace can happen.

To reply without anger, need authentic empathy.
What am I missing?

What is Real Education

What is REAL Education?
Books,
Scores,
Career ...

I remember, during PG final semester, a variety of puzzles with missing pieces scattered before us.
ABCD, the four friends, self-conscious with expectations and potential possibilities.
Aspiration
Breakthrough
Consequence
Decision

The circumstances favored ABD, during earlier semesters. Hostel and Mess life created interdependent passages and they overcame conflict, the existential challenges called Exams.

C, the consequence was left out stranded in circumstances, with four options, for the expectations, whenever she came across Exams.
Equal
Less
More

Opposite
She was always LESS with her outcomes.
Always miserable, defined, and confined.
Day scholar.

The Breakthrough with Decision managed to cultivate Aspiration and dissolve the tensions within Consequence to appear for the final semester.
Togetherness (ABCD) wins.
C topped in that semester.

Adds value, share values. REAL education is more than Mastery over scores.
Scores are numbers.
In fact, we no longer read our numbers. We read broken words when we look back to read our books of togetherness. We read meanings that we value feelings, friendship. The parts come together to become WHOLE.

Where all WIN.

What is REAL Education, for you?

The Suns are Stuck

Renovation of the building is impossible.
We are tired of her negativity, A concluded.
I have nothing to add or subtract in the meeting. The hope
of getting together always depends on the negative aspect
of everything.

K, cannot accept any changes and she has reasons from
the past for not contributing to the repair.

We want a beautiful, happy future.

We are the sum of all the families.

But our mind is programmed with the past. It needs an
instant linear solution.

K has to contribute.

K, will not.

Hope eclipsed.
The direction set to the expectations along with K's past.

Vision is now, not Aspirational rather the vision is now
Expectation.

The direction identified.

The mission statement of the house declares,
The purpose. The Blocks with fresh oxygen grew larger.

Something inside me wanted to react. Inform, please keep
away from the past. But the Sun got stuck in my throat.
I visited A doctor; A Friend
All can see but could not guide.

Decided to sleep.
Thousands of Suns in mind space appeared floating with
melancholy.

The wind within whispered to me.

Sun is the epitome of light.
All Suns are stuck within, eclipsed by cloudy past.
They are not fiery enough to produce light.

Are we aware of not enough fusion happening inside to be
light?

PV = Constant

Sir, why people are afraid of Chemistry?
My gaze was limited to Gas law derivation by a student.
From nowhere my thoughts jumped into the orbit of
introspection, groping for answers.

Q & A is a game we play to reach solutions in
conventional learning.
I stayed silent.

Sir, if you don't mind, can I ask you a personal question?
 Yes.

What was your score during your B.Sc Examination?

55%, second class, this was easy for me to answer.

He looked at me in disbelief.
Maybe his curiosity is pushing him to ask, second class?

I felt vulnerable.

Marks are the irreducible parameter of a student.
Marks often create mental pain.

Successful in a job, yet the suffering of the past seems to

exist.

Felt the PRESSURE with the judgments of others.

P × V=CONSTANT,
started to dance.

Pressure is stress within, reduces when perspective increases.
The narrative within can create expanded Volume to reduce stress.
I smiled at him.
>Why worry?
>I will guide you to success.

What is Success?
The CONSTANT (inclusiveness) in every aspect of life, EVERY MOMENT, is a success.
When we do not accept, say uncertainty, we generate fear.
With acceptance, it's an adventure, it's a success.

Accepting perspectives is SUCCESS.

Transcend MOMENTS.

Creative Dance

Ma, why did you cut my hair?
I am looking like a boy.

Oisi, feeling isolated. She is self-conscious about her looks.

Her mother is simple and straight.

You attracted the outcome. You tried to color your hair with lipstick. The careless-craft using fevicols is also the reason for your hair fall.
Her mother feels short hair will reduce hair fall. So, hair was shortened.

Emotional honesty, a skill, required.
My resistance to shortening my hair came to the surface.
Her mother too shared her instance with me.

Oisi, is worried about her Rabindra Dance performance.
Her immediate want is to purchase a wick for her from Amazon. I tried to mitigate her expectation.

Oscillating between Oisi and her Mom needed a dose of spiritual vaccination. Humor, play, story-telling are essential to pull her up.

The doctor advised us not to worry.
All summed up to her strength.
The strength is determined by the energetic dimension within. Our acceptance generated enough self-esteem within her. And was less available to external influences.

She and her granny managed to un-pluck two ponytails from a cap, clipped the same with a hairband.

Look and likeness changed.
Dancer and dance for us was now a celebration.

Self-infused responsibility from Oisi changed the climate altogether.

What is Success

What do you write in writing challenges? My daughter inquired.
>I write my experiences, my thoughts.
Can I help you with writing?
>How?
Sharing with you some idea about what you can write?
>Ok, share.

This conversation led me to share about the recently concluded monthly power writer's contest. The topic was YOUR DEFINITION OF SUCCESS.

Success, for her, is about +1 and -1.

I was intrigued to hear her.

I asked her to explain.

She said, if you are sad, you need light, you need to open and so add ONE (+1).
If you are joyful, reduce ONE, stay grounded.
Success is about balance.
With this, she left, but my thoughts kept repeating to understand.
-1   0   +1

I included BALANCE as, ZERO.

It is in equilibrium and restfulness, a feeling of satisfaction happens.

Recycling the definition of Success led me to the beauty of another kind.

The moment we consciously harness the energy, the moment we compartmentalize with the definition, we lose the possibilities of spontaneous life it(moment) holds.

Celebrate the creative moment.

Success is a Celebration of the prepared moment.

It's BALANCE

What is Success for you?

Read, Review, Relive

What book are you reading?
The voice of my co-passenger interrupted my attention.
This book is a memoir of a Bengali Publisher, I said

How is the writing?
Very beautiful, it is the journey of BECOMING from a humble beginning.

Read his writing and feel nothing great about it, he showcased difference.

Is this statement trying to engage me in a dialogue or truly trying to challenge my use of the term "beautiful"?
Let me not judge. Often to initiate conversation one may use differences.
Here silence is the best dialogue to avoid controversies.

I kept reading and outlining the part I have finished. Since I was sure this is a beginning of communication which will venture my depth around reading.

The Bengali literature has died. You will not enjoy reading any authors. He declared confidently.
I am not a passionate reader of Bengali literature but my idea differs.

How do I influence?
To answer someone with confidence needs preparedness.

Which other authors of the present time you have read?
...
For the rest of our journey, the two minds with our thoughts continued expanding our inner space and likewise reflecting our nature.

Realizing only light can dispel darkness.
Be light, burn yourself.
Read, Review, Relive.
Assimilate.

CONSILIO ET ANIMO

2018, at College Library. A, my school friend, popped up as a WhatsApp message.

Transported to 1992, standard VIII, before our English language exams. The St. Vincent's High and Technical School motto CONSILIO ET ANIMO became a means to influence our English teacher, Mr. Gabriel.
The motto is the satellite, launched by the rocket, A, into the orbit of discussion of scoring.

Whatever essay comes insert, CONSILIO ET ANIMO? A stated confidently

I murmured and felt curious.

I asked A, how do I do?
Mischief all around rolled.
But, A connected.
Use DEDICATION, DEVOTION, & DISCIPLINE within your essay. This is what it means.
The College Librarian Sir intervened in my memories.
Good Morning Sir, your 1st Year students asking for books.
I have asked them to wait and consult you.

It's 8.30 am and my class is from 9.45 am.
I will meet them at class.

Do you think they will come to your class?
This is a beautiful question.

Do I add value to their life?
Do the quality of our life synergetic with each other?
Why do the fundamentals of interaction stand as a question?

I asked myself.

If you want to transform this ideal day into reality what would you do?
Make them feel visible. Create my own favoring environment.
Initiate conversation.
CONSILIO ET ANIMO
Choose Devotion.
Rest will follow.

How do our students see us

I remember, in 2016, K stood out as a student, pursuing her Master's at our College. She was obedient, and wonderful at everything.
A friend of hers called me to inform me that K's father passed away due to Covid. Reality exposed the vulnerability of dependence.

The network of friends trying some means to manage the crisis is an effort to lift the family. Receiving Whatsapp messages led my attention to the crisis.
Sir, K, with her sister, and mother is depressed.
Need some way to income.
Any project, Sir?

How our students see us is different from how we see ourselves.

They are trying to reach out to dependable someone. Prepared with an idea, with a form to mitigate the situation.

 I have only words to offer.
Need is work, that can push her fears and support her.

Hopeful words will feed her thinking.

Thinking to Action is an onward journey.
Emotional Motivation may appear as a catalyst, comforting
but will not provide direction.
Need is discipline, Goal.

She has skills that need to be capitalized on to generate
wealth.
I have some offerings to expand the mindset and look
beyond Chemistry.

The external voices must connect with her internal voice
for her transformation.

I messaged her.
Her reply, Ok sir, gave me relief.

Car Called Self Development

How will you spend time with my mother? My daughter inquired.
Presently driving a car called, SELF-DEVELOPMENT, taking my daughter on a ride.

As X-ray diffraction method is a useful tool and technique to elucidate the fascinating structural world within an atom. Likewise, conversations illuminate the layers beyond the immediate surface.

The answer, dad. She seemed intrigued to listen.

>Thinking! Can you help me with more simple ways?

You need to write.
> Write, what?

Write 3 Tasks you want to do together with, other than watching a film.
> Walk walk exercise,
> Lunch, as usual,
>Watch Rani Rashmoni, a TV serial,
Outline tried conveyed.

There is no common time where I fit? she laments.

>Lunch, dinner, and story, as usual, I said.

Dad, Your LOVE is invisible.

Write,
How can you show your, LOVE?
How do you see the person?
Why do you love the person?
Do you love your webinar more or the person?

Step down for a few days from your self-development activity, dad.
Balance the structure.

In biology, STRUCTURE is crucial to FUNCTION.
The structure is almost everything in Chemistry, especially when chemical reactions (conversations) influences biology (LIFE).

Now, Is SELF DEVELOPMENT exclusive?

The need is a favorable environment.

What is your opinion?

Productivity

Reading AmarChitraKatha with my daughter led us into the world of Sant Ravidas. The Indian mystic of the Bhakti Movement (15th-16th C.E). The idea of untouchables, prejudice of caste was prevalent during his time.

He suffered so many hurdles, Dad?

Yes, he suffered but his struggles led him to surmount the impossible heights with his Bhakti.

What is Bhakti? Oishi inquired.
Bhakti, is personal branding, meeting with, the ONE.
He was a social reformer but first, he was the person who influenced himself most. Realized OWNSELF.

Who is a Social Reformer?
The person who has the solution to reduce the basic blocks(limiting beliefs) within people (society) of his time are called social reformers.

Do we have blocks, dad?
Yes, we all have.
To reduce blocks we read, write, listen to good things and we create a space of productivity.

Productivity?

Productivity is hidden within us all eclipsed by blocks.

The one who is sensitive to the pain of self will connect others effortlessly along his journey. Empathetic self creates a Productive Brand of own kind.

Adding value creates the brand.

We are the sum total of our productive brand (mindset), of our time.

What is personal branding/productivity for me?

Where is my Attention, Focus, Energy flowing?

Productivity will meet me there.

Life is Fun and Work

Life is not Fun, Life only works. Oishi cried sadly
What happened? I asked

Mom is always with her rules and ruler. She complained
But, she never hits you, why worry?

I don't feel valued, Dad.
If you focus too much on self-worth, you will get isolated.
Follow her rules.

She always says study.
OK, study.

Why do you study?
Now, it is my work. The official purpose of my work is to
satisfy my students; unofficially I have to satisfy own self.
So I study and enjoy.

You enjoy and study. I don't enjoy it. and I don't study.
Good logic, I said.

I enjoy painting, I feel alive when I draw.
FUN and WORK need connection. How do I find interest
in her?
How do I engage her with work?

Work is the tool that helps us grow. We can feel stress, but growth manifests when we work in a direction. Her mother has a way with work.

Include writings in your drawings. Writing is communication. The more you write, the more you will realize the FUN in your work.
Find the Unseen New in YOU. I said.

WORK helps one to give what the world wants from us, FUN has the promise to deliver what one can give to others.

In a world that celebrates alignment, Work can increasingly make the individual invisible.
Fun has the potential of realizing the possibility of the individual, to be VISIBLE.
How do we balance?

What is SCIENCE

Formal training in science is useful to design life along the direction. It creates a system which when followed, efforts manifests into results. Promises get delivered.

I don't like science, dad.
Ma, I don't want to be a doctor as well. I want to be a writer. Our 9-year-old daughter concluded.

Her interest in Science is no more.

A Chemist within me reflects.

Chemists build molecules, which get tested later. They visualize the distribution of electron cloud within the molecule and accordingly choose a reactant to realize the desired product.

My wife is disturbed by my thought fullness with no activities related to my child.
We need her to appreciate the essence of observation and understanding through science.

As a father what you sacrifice is more important than what you do?
I didn't follow. I whispered.

You are on a journey of resourcefulness, missing out on your own resourceful daughter.

The mystery, magic, meaning each object holds it's for you to inspire through observation, creating relation. What is science? It's for you to convey.

Need is your Energy, Attention, Focus.

Our time.

One thought knocking ...

What is SCIENCE?

Appendix

73   What is SCIENCE?